I Dreamed a World

Colleen Anderson

LVP
PUBLICATIONS

"There is no ignoring the choir of color dreamed in Colleen Anderson's new collection. Infinite goddesses evolve in her poetry, helping all find the bitter-sweet thoughts hidden in the preconception we call Waking. Journeying in her poetry always makes me want to write & dream evermore!"
—Linda D. Addison, award-winning author, HWA Lifetime Achievement Award recipient and SFPA Grand Master

"Inspired by the mystical aspects of human experience, Colleen Anderson has given us her own version of archetypal feminine tales and brought her own unique touch to these versions of female characters from a spectrum of traditional mythologies (and a few modern ones). She leads us through the old-growth forests of human legend, wandering in haunted shadows and in sun-dappled clearings. From the title poem: "I dreamed a world where ... the only spell is one of making." *—F. J. Bergmann, Elgin & Rhysling Award winner*

"With I Dreamed A World we have an impressive collection spanning four decades of imaginative verse that will serve as a wonderful introduction to new readers and surely delight those already familiar with Colleen Anderson's thoughtful and wide-ranging poetry. Many familiar figures of myth and fairy tale are re-imagined here, challenging our conventional understanding and how we might think of these women in the futures ahead. Whether Medusa and Rapunzel or Talesen and mermaids, these provocative poems deliver compelling ways to view each of them anew!" *—Bryan Thao Worra, Lao Minnesotan Poet Laureate, Science Fiction and Fantasy Poetry Association President*

"This is a breath-taking collection from Aurora and Rhysling nominee Colleen Anderson. Across the considered and considerable span of these poems, Anderson reconfigures the role of and gives new voice to heroines and archetypes from mythology, fairy tale and popular culture. She shows us Persephone stained into heady knowledge by the seeds and juice of the pomegranate; she conjures a rapport between Rapunzel and Medusa ("Day by day, like obsessive schoolgirls / they compared notes, talked of their confines"); she elucidates for us that "Snow White was a victim of conspiracies / when a prophetic mirror dared to dictate the future". In this wide-ranging yet cleverly sequential book, Colleen Anderson makes us privy to the revelation that "Fairy tales are the memories of gods long gone" and recasts our inherited fantastical culture through a feminist lens. This is a major addition to the genre poetry canon."—*Allen Ashley, British Fantasy Award winner and Former President of the British Fantasy Society*

"I Dreamed a World by Colleen Anderson creates an effortlessly detailed engine of invention both thrilling and daunting. Dramatic monologues by Leda, Athena, Cinderella, Shahrazad, and Snow White, for instance, paint a grisly scene of abuse that gives way to resistance and female empowerment. This inclination to find hope or strength characterizes much of Anderson's work. Unlike Persephone, you surely will feel an "intemperate heat" as you enjoy this collection that balances the fantastic with the practical — and counterweights frustration and despair with hard-won joy."
—*LindaAnn LoSchiavo, A Route Obscure and Lonely, Elgin Award winner*

Cover Art by Stefan Keller, Cover Design by LVP Publications, © 2022 LVP Publications

I Dreamed A World Copyright © 2022, Colleen Anderson and LVP Publications

All rights reserved. No part of this book may be reproduced in any form, including in print, electronic form or by mechanical means, without written permission from the publisher, author or individual copyright holder except for in the case of a book reviewer, who may quote brief passages embedded in and as part of an article or review.

This is a work of fiction. Names, characters, businesses, places, events and incidents are either the products of the author's imagination or used in a fictitious manner. Any resemblance to actual persons, living or dead, or actual events is purely coincidental.

Lycan Valley Press Publications
1625 E 72nd St STE 700 PMB 132
Tacoma, Washington 98404
United States of America

Printed in the United States of America

First Edition

ISBN: 978-1-64562-941-2

To women in the past and in the present, to those whose voices were heard and those who could not speak. To telling the real tales, for not having to earn their place in the world but have the right of being themselves, without being something else. To all my sisters, mythic and real and human.

And to Marie Ferris. We've been through thick and thin for a long time, and are different beings whose friendship continues through all these changes. Thank you for your support, always.

I Dreamed a World

Contents

Introduction by Angela Yuriko Smith	1
Geomystica	3
Queen Of Heaven And Earth	8
Of The Corn	10
Persephone Dreams	12
Finding Dionysus	14
The First Taste	15
Illuminating Thoughts	17
Father's Child	19
Visitation	21
New Age	23
Rapunzel And Medusa	25
Medusa	29
Cleopatra	31
Morrigan's Song	32
The Vernal Queen	34
A Question Of The Grail	36
The Enlightened	38
Safe-Keeping	40
The Loving Cup	43
Spinning Wheel	44
Spirit Of Heart	46

WITCH MOON	48
BY THE LIGHT OF THE MOON	50
PENNED BY MY HAND	51
BOOK OF SHADOWS	53
BROKEN WORDS	55
IN FELINE GRACE	57
LOREENA	59
THE BRIAR WITCH	61
THE HEDGE WITCH	63
THE STORM WITCH	65
THE SAND WITCH	68
WHAT GOLDILOCKS LEARNED	70
A GOOD CATCH	72
MERMAID'S COMB	74
MERMAID	76
THE MERMAID	78
HEART OF GLASS	80
I DREAMED A WORLD	83
CINDERELLA'S PUMPKIN	87
SNOW WHITE'S APPLES	91
THE LOOKING GLASS	94
LEARNING TO RUN	97
CHARMED	99
SHAHRAZAD: CAPTIVE PASSION	101
AS I SLEEP	104
UNINVITED	106
A STRANGE ATTRACTION	107
THE TRAVELER	109
VOODOO DOLL	111
PATCHWORK GIRL	112

THE BEETLE WIFE	114
TALESEN'S TRAP 2115-2135: MAIE	116
TALESEN'S TRAP 2203-2213: THENA	118
TALESEN'S TRAP 2272-2378: DEMEY	120
TALESEN'S TRAP 3480: LAZU	122
NOCTURNE EXPIRE	124
THE PRICE	126
OH YOU!	129
BY THE END	131
ACKNOWLEDGEMENTS	133
CREDITS	135
ABOUT THE AUTHOR	139

INTRODUCTION

By Angela Yuriko Smith

Reader be wary. Here there be magic.

Take heed. This is not cardboard sleight-of-hand and rabbits-in-a-hat magic. This is the deep, dark and powerful essence of the feminine. This is starshine cascading from the heavens, singing in the darkened glade to a wink of moon magic. Cosmic femininity, feral beauty and maternal power merge on the page in complex incantations of verse and syntax.

From the roots of time, Colleen Anderson has assembled an assortment of goddesses, witches and myth to tell lyrical stories of what it means to tap into the dark feminine. Misunderstood since the first sunrise, she captures what it means to be woman from innocence to passion, motherhood to immortality.

From FATHER'S CHILD:

> From within—fearless Metis opened her thighs
> in blood she birthed me
> then fed me milk and words

Every mother can feel the weighted pain behind these words, feel the maternal conflict of fierce love. Anderson is fearless as she confronts our duality and mystique.

One of my favorite poems of the collection touches on this contrast. In RAPUNZEL AND MEDUSA the similarities and differences of the two myths are compared, but instead of a dry commentary on their similarities, Anderson draws them together by their differences in love. She calls to mind how women bond. When hurt, we draw together and strengthen each other. Bruised hearts bond into sisterhoods and covens.

A reader will not want to rush through this grimoire of poetry. Each splash of ink is a summonings to the inamorata within us. Each jot is a testament to the gentle tempest that waits to be unleashed. This is a work I will enjoy continuously. It is a tonic for the disadvantaged, a balm for weeping queens, a justification for the sorceress in us all.

Reader be wary. Here there be magic.

Geomystica

In the first clench of colorless space
cold so hard it cuts like glass
air so harsh it falls as ice
Life so empty it is yet to be noticed

In this nothing, this lack of breath
a swirl of ebon upon empty color
a gathering
indrawing
waiting of time

A pucker—the cosmos folds and buckles
torn, it whirls and shreds
locked in embrace
scattered forever

Pulled and drawn
woven and raveled
woken and silenced
sunset and dawn

Colleen Anderson

Where nothing was
yet everything is
a congealing of seconds to matter
weaves mind with the thought
the time to be soon
the when to be ever

Hands claw the fabric
tugging with sound and motions unknown
she reaches and gathers
the dust and the moisture
she rolls in the warmth
garners the essence
then lets it float

The solitary goddess looks on her disc
With thumbs and lined fingers
she rounds it out
presses in seeds
Atoms—beginnings
breaths in reserve for moments to be

Pleased with her image
she jumps on the sphere
and dances it
beneath her feet
she twirls—wanton flurry of forces
a blur to the unborn seers of time
the ball in attraction
whirls in her wake

I DREAMED A WORLD

The dance endures the coal-dark void
spinning
twirling
sweat sprays out
spattering space with luminous light
lighted now, evolution and change

She stops
the orb revolves
so swiftly—everything seems to stand still
but the goddess, unfinished continues to dance
stomps her foot in primal joy
and frustration
she stomps again in response

The vibration
reaction sets the clay smoldering
heating and flaring with elemental force

Fire—she breathes perfumed breath
fans the flames
feeds her desire
warms the world's frozen glaze
builds the beginning, the heat of life
the rebirth of lava
destructive melting
the inspiring hearth fire
warm candlelight
the brightness of sight

Colleen Anderson

Air—she claps in delight at the ball
sends it orbiting away on an elliptical path
it rotates along a spiral she weaves
the clap of thunder
thrill of sound
the vibrational wave
the seed-floating breeze
sigh of the living
the breath of meaning

Water—she cries as it flows in furrows
the world compacting, her hands slick mud
mold mounds as she spits out dirt
the eternal ices
thrashing downpour
the dew-swept land
the flow of the womb
surge of blood
the trickle of tears

Earth—she laughs
the precipice quakes
her toes root stone
she gyrates the thrum
the rooting trees
bursting seed
strength of bone
flesh and blood and dirt
and weight of more to come

I DREAMED A WORLD

Spirit—she whispers in the ears of all beings
in the leaves of young shoots
the bark of all trees
small scuttling crawlers
swimmers of seas
she laughs and runs—dancing the sky
making—unmaking everything now
he then she then we and on
All that is possible

She flickers in and out and through
the blooming of we
the revisions of you
dancing time's feel
re-creation and permanence
temporal vines

Again she spins
and again she twirls
and again she creates and unravels
moments sublime

She shatters conceptions
all beginning in you
ending in me

Queen Of Heaven And Earth

In the beginning
there was nothing
Then in hot plasma bursts
came the Angel of time

Mother of us all
birthing planets to seed with souls
Some of those planets–
her testing grounds for serious thought
others, the whimsy of idle dreams

She nurtures them until maturity
where all deeds come to fruit
Some have the flesh of beauty
but the taste is bitter truth
Many that are bitten
turn sour in the gut of testing

I DREAMED A WORLD

Some of those souls
bloom hot and fragrant
Then she blows them into falling stars
cupped in her gentle, iced hands
waiting, waiting to plant her garden anew

Dormant planets, expectant souls
in her pockets rubbing edges
She wanders through the infinite realm
testing, touching

Through the halls of blue-white marble
past the pillars of history
her hollow footsteps
echo on the bones of those who sleep

Of The Corn

Kore's Innocence

This is my promise
As you have sown the grain
so shall I know its growing
I will know every veined leaf
hue of every flower

I coax the crocus to unfurl its leaves
the poppy to bloom
new even as it withers
I stroke the shoots of the iris
bring its breath to Apollo

> I have never learned difference
> You and I moving together
> I know always what was
> what is and what will be

I DREAMED A WORLD

But at times
when you are tending the grain
when Apollo sleeps
I sleep
I dream I still sleep in the dark
amongst the flowers
Their hidden roots
reach
down
where I have fallen
a crushed poppy
a decayed bloom
a faded color

Then earth gapes black
and I tremble cold
awake to find the fields flowering

Persephone Dreams

Awakening

Dayblooms endlessly unfurl
violets, roses, irises
a rainbow bridge to walk
I pluck blossoms knowing others
always take their place

Content in the bower
of my mother's verdant bosom
I sleep under sun's reflection
not feeling my intemperate heat

In the shadows of my dreams
a cool shade stirs me
to wake
      to look
           to touch beneath the bloom
feel the sturdy stalk
      the biting thorn that snares me

I Dreamed a World

I taste the drop of blood as darkness unfolds
wraps petals about me

Awaking in full flower
I imagine nothing's different until
I reach below lulling scents
to furrow the moist earth
and grasp narcissus by musky roots

Finding Dionysus

Descent

When first I was thrown to Erebos
cold shocked my drowning soul
ice lips numbed me
then warmed me to a different sigh

I watched the swirling mists of shades
dipped my hand
the current altered
bringing a flow to his realm

I had never known
what vessel his words uncorked
how diving deeper would fill me
with a taste for something more
nor how the blood-colored seeds I bit
would stain my heart burgundy
a full cup that I tasted
as he poured

The First Taste

Persephone Awakes

It is the pomegranate I remember

The flesh so taut
glistened as he pulled it apart
I wanted—more entrancing than the rarest flower
But I was afraid, not knowing nearly enough
I could not stare at shadows so I reached for
 warmth

That first seed drew darkness into itself
quenched a thirst I had not known
Blood thundered through the halls of my veins
The first bloom, a thundershower
when everything opens up

The second seed was not so black
I wanted to taste again
the juices beading his fingers—I sucked;

I chewed the sweet pulp
felt it fill my need
sting my tongue
and burnish my lips to ruby

The third seed burst with crimson abandon
I knew there would be more
to taste his nectar
The pomegranate's juice flowed freely
A stygian river deep blood red
staining my legs his mouth
I breathed in its heady scent
no longer a pale bloom

With that dying blush
I applied strange symbols
to his body and mine
Tattooed with knowing
the cold black knowing
the warm red knowing
of where I had gone
of what I was
and what I would be
as many ways as there are red seeds

Illuminating Thoughts

Psyche's Remorse

Each night as cool and black as weighted silk
he came to me, enveloped me, loved me
Each night he kissed me, whispered
then faded with the stars

I awoke to daylight in a fever
devoured the sight of every man
sure that one would claim me
waiting silently for my dream

The marketplace gossips laughed
A hidden husband who came in dreams?
How could I be a proper woman?
How could he support a family?

I never felt his gaze
Yet at night his heat consumed me

I began to burn in darkness
a brand never doused

Blinded by my need
I revealed my lover to the light
Winged, warm, too pure for mortal form
Eros awoke, scolded me, flew from my embrace

I searched for him, followed him
suffered feats to be with him
and in the end the love I kindled
burned me through and through

I could not stay with people
after Eros took my heart
I only wanted love
not to rival a god's splendor

Was it knowing godhood
he had tried to hide from me
or the knowledge of my lost humanity
that I have learned to mourn?

Father's Child

Athena's Choice

From within—fearless Metis opened her thighs
in blood she birthed me
then fed me milk and words
Metis told me he had swallowed us
hoping to keep our wisdom
she was content to wait and plan
knew I would do as I choose

And so I chose
he could not swallow destiny
and I battled with words
speared his every thought
knowing full well my power
in my father

He conceived an idea, words, a gender
tried to swallow the counsel of women
tried to digest me before I opposed

I did not spring from his head
More my anger boiled too long
that brought my release

I countered until I won my way
out he called for Hephaestus
bright ingenious Hephaestus
who swung his mighty axe
split the head of Zeus in two

Out of that duality
I strode forth

Visitation

Leda's Lament

A swan settles on my dream
in the heavy silence of the night

I gasp, bound by colorless feathers
I am as pale as the moon

Beyond this heaving
Past the down that drowns
my mouth my ears my eyes
I remember

> laughter from dancers' lips
> their feet stomp musky grapes
> green vines in their hair,
> the air scented with wine

Pinions cleave me
open wounds
pulsing, red, swollen

The eyes glint
the beak dips in
Once, twice and my heart is gone

Numbed by trumpetings of a swan
I cannot shake the feeling

As it lifts
I am hollow to my bones
breathless in flight

New Age

Nervous shadows pull her skin,
hide in fleshy crevices
while her splotchy bark hands
crab over the loom
setting the last of the pattern.
The dried blood flames
lick close the embers,
while wind moans its age
and tosses snow at the door.
Her bones creak in chorus
to loom and door, as a sound,
like glaciers snapping,
rattles through her raisined lips.

Midnight
Wind has gone to hide;
Snow sleeps hugging the hut.
Moon, alive as cracking eggs,
shines silver on her tired, shriveled form.

Morning pushes brightly through the downy
    blanket,
batting clouds on home,
and sets to causing snow to cry
in memory of past storms.
She glides to her loom,
picking spring threads that tangle gaily,
while her young root hands pat them apart.
Light pushes cowering dark to the cracks
and brushes over her velvet cream face.
The loom is large, but her hands will weave,
like birds nesting,
and set the new pattern she creates.

Rapunzel And Medusa

Theirs was a relationship born of need
each banished from society's gentler refrains

Rapunzel, a prize, trophy, prisoner
sequestered from all eyes
hoarded by a witch
who coveted pretty baubles
So her hair grew in defiance
blindly searching like sun-seeking vines
wheaten bounty, golden filaments
for any chance of escape into the world

Framed by her window
her gaze traveled past horizons
beyond the limits of town borders
as she peered deep within herself
repainting captive worlds from her bower

Medusa, scapegoat, monster, victim
hidden, a pariah of vision
if any could have spoken having looked upon her
they would have told of beauty
the corona about her head
the scintillating glint of sinuous bodies
endless sliding ropes polished copper, viridian, topaz
a frozen rainbow waiting to spill forth

Her serpentine hair constantly sought
tongues tasting two ways, a path back to society
or into the arms of anyone without a heart of stone
who could hold her close
each snake head's little red eyes watching
the state of her realm in stasis

Eventually, through wind-born seeds
breathy birds landing for a rest
the restless bustling of beetles
flies and insects of secret and forbidden places
Rapunzel and Medusa came to hear
of each other's predicament

They sent messages back and forth
with the aid of inhuman couriers
written on small scraps of parchment
flat seed pods, or the bones of fowl
for where enchantment and curses exist
so do other means of magic

I DREAMED A WORLD

Day by day, like obsessive schoolgirls
they compared notes, talked of their confines
limited worldview and the passions
of their hearts, a galaxy yet unexplored
but only hinted at, a fate of destiny
Their distant friendship bloomed
grew to fruit though neither had ever tasted
of the other's nectar

A love took root and held them fast
Rapunzel's tresses always seeking through the
    light
Medusa's snakes burrowing through the
    underworld
nurtured by tears and promises
whispered into the air

A shoot's tender head raised itself
first small then exceedingly resilient
it climbed onto walls, tumbled over wells
crept along the sills of every window
in every town

Slowly it spread as it drew them together
the vine's conduit allowed a vibratory touch
a way to let the other know
she was truly alive

The serpents sent their sibilant vows
forever twined, a force that reached beyond

all cages, boundaries or restrictions
like Abelard and Heloise
isolated yet together
Rapunzel and Medusa endured forever
no longer alone

Medusa

She unbraids every hissing filament
Sets her hair to writhing
One cannot help but be a viper when many heads
    are at war
A mind of her own would have been nice

Her biting remarks
Poisonous words
There was no way to know when she would lash
    out
Blind with fear or hate or an instinctual mating
    need

She tried to tame them
Smooth with gels
Hide under a Gucci scarf
Feed them the sweetest nectars

When really all they wanted
A place to burrow, a dark hole

It would have saved them stony looks
If any had tried to understand the language of
    snakes

She once thought to cut them off
But knew the pain would drive her mad
Send them squirming inside in hatred
Isolation and self-loathing

So she endures the constant undulations
Of an untamed mind
Knowing much better she be thought a gorgon
Than to wear her heart on her sleeve

Cleopatra

Have you ever felt the hunger
As if ants crawl in your belly
As if an abyss consumes your soul

Have you ever felt the sting
As if an asp bites your breast
As if the world is ending in your heart

Have you ever felt the kiss
As if lotus petals brush your cheek
As if the gods caress your thoughts

With each one I received the rest
A bounty that drains me
My blood seeps into the earth
Wraps me, feeds me so that I may rise again

Morrigan's Song

Breathe in the moist air, smell the land within it
hear the movement of trees and animals all
    around
far away, in daylight, the eagle's call pins the sky
deer ghost through the glen
ravens call into the night as they settle into
    sleep
You are before a cubby hole, a warren, a den.

I become ink on the spill of darkness
tearing through the shroud
soaring over battlefields, beds of the slain
I pluck the souls and carry them back
Hear not pleas of salvation and supplication
I am a howl, a hungry cat, a carrion crow.

You stand before Oweynagat, the cave of the
    cats
mist shrouds your sight, rain shivers your soul

cold bites deeper than any bitter tears
you will travel far beneath earth's skin
the cavern's dark mouth opens, takes you in
It is a hole, a pit, an abyss.

Dripping water echoes, your only anchor
as you slide into the otherworld
on your back, unable to change your destiny
light dims as you glide deeper, frozen
you are alone in the earth's damp belly
You are a corpse, a worm, an embryo.

In complete blackness an ember glows
golden light grows, becomes stronger, enticing
you do not need eyes to see the brightness
that gathers and spins, like the galaxy
you do not need hands to touch it
You are a spark, a flame, a spirit.

In between the beginnings of life and death
I anchor you in this humid enclosure, a cauldron
in the darkest times I stir memory and remorse
mixing strength into the vessel in which you
    reside
tasting all as you are made and remade
you are a silhouette, a shadow, a shade
I collect you, I cannot save you, I am the
    Morrigan.

The Vernal Queen

He came to me.
I was still young,
growing like new shoots.
I enraptured him,
rooted a King–
a kingdom,
coaxed forth his budding purpose–
canopied the Summer King
in his ripe and fecund land.
The fruition of his power,
prosperity.
Left unharvested, the decay seeped in.
All withered.
I was the Fall to the Winter King.
His wisdom, having grown past its day,
I passed him by,
consigned Arthur to the dying time–
abandoned the Winter King
to the bone-white realm.

I DREAMED A WORLD

To preserve my Spring
I searched for budding youth.
His strength and perfection, shooting forth,
my love for Lancelot seeded him
toward his summering.
I grew anew with greening life.
In eagerness, in youth
he came to me.

A Question Of The Grail

Always,
Bewailing their loss, they come to me
Lady, we cannot find the Grail
It is forever lost

Is it?
Yes, yes
Hidden through veiled centuries
We search everywhere
There is no place it could be

There isn't?
No, no it's gone
It will never be found

Who last held it?
Why, Arthur's court—or Parsival, that is
Beheld it, then both disappeared

You know why?
Man proved unworthy
The Grail is forsaken 'til such a man returns

A man?
And so they quest
Always, for a jewelled cup, tempestuous metals
They complain to me
Grieve while not perceiving
What it is that's really lost

I know
Never asking of me
Where the Grail is?
I know

What it is?
I am

The Enlightened

She was the White
    blissful as light unsullied by dawn
    undaunted by a turning age
    when miracles were birthed
years unblemished by history
virtue untainted by touch

    She fought for a tranquil soil
    with charity, an open heart
    where saints feared to meddle

Guenavar, his queen, steadfast, unbreachable
she had no chance, treading mankind's world
confronting herself and one whose utmost loyalty
threw temptation at her very stepfall

And the other

I Dreamed a World

She was the Fey
    black as night caressed by stars
    twinkling shadows of an older age
    when light and dark were married
eons made of mystery
flowers sprouting from the crypt

    She rioted for chaotic whim
    everchanging, growing terrain
    containing capricious gods

Morgause, sister, opposing, unreachable
she grasped a task beyond her vision
defying reason sure to be scorned
for baring all faults, even his

He was the sun about which
they revolved
resolving little
In the face of his duality
balanced by opposites
he burned to a husk
between flesh and soul

Safe-Keeping

The Deep Sleep
Arthur's still form rests
Until his wisdom is roused
    His need, our need
    His death, our life
We watch over him
    We, the protected
Ready for Fate's call
    The fateful call
    We shan't let it
    Will We?
We shall awaken the Golden King
When the dark times return
    We can quell those times
    can't We?
Now We administer again
The bite of the thorn
That ensures sleep
    Sleep, sleep,
    but not for us

No, never
    he can't wake
We must keep vigil
So our land may live
    It still lives,
    doesn't it
    Above,
    green, hale
Until the crisis
    He won't wake
    Our King
    We reign
    this cold realm
    this crypt
He cannot foreshadow
the foretold doom
    We keep His sleep
    It won't happen
    Can't, can it?
    No
    No, safe

Arthur's long rest thwarts
the two-fold prophecy
    No doom, no King
    No King, no end
He does not know
    No end in sight
    to see again
    green lands

We—
>   I—grow tired
>   Of white walls
>   White robes
>   White
>   > Sleep

The Loving Cup

White breast, cupped
Moonface
Face each other
Travel the valley past two moons
To darker groves
Moisture touches
Tufted bushes
Before coursing
Into the secret cavern

Cupped there
Coupled in tight embrace
A sea of life fills the chalice
From beneath

The never emptying cup
flows and fills
reflects a full moon

A vessel of tides
That ebbs and flows

Spinning Wheel

Her handprint is upon
this wheel
I touch the coarse-gritted furrows
sift through bones, ripening seeds

The wheel turns
shadowed indentations
where her fingers pressed
faintest tender green reaches
toward the sun

She spins the wheel
around its center
I kneel, press my nose into
moist soil, rainbow blooms
musty decay, tangy aromas
entwine within me

She pulls the wheel
through the season

I DREAMED A WORLD

I lick at fruity nectar
sliding down my throat
it fills me with light
I do not eat the bruises
push them back into the earth

I hear the wheel
grinding onward
turning lightly rhythmic rumbling
her voice silently whispers
there are no words
for that which is beyond
words
she shows me as I roll

Upon this wheel
this turning earth
I will grow and die
and learn to live again

Spirit Of Heart

I am the velvet deer,
nostrils quivering at invading scents,
who bolts as you try to hunt me
take me for your dinner—to savor.

I am the whispery butterfly,
alight on nectared blooms,
who flutters away as you swing your net
to snare me for your display.

I am the emerging bud,
flowering on heat-kissed wind,
and turn to deeds aloft
before your touch can pluck my life.

I am the molten brook,
sprinting over dappled rocks,
and trickles through the dam of your beliefs
where you would hold me- stagnate my life.

I DREAMED A WORLD

I am the free spirit,
eternal life and wandering,
to choose and love what I please—
not captured by your selfish love.

Witch Moon

We are witches, women all
women worshipping the moon
every moon watching timeless wisdom
wisdom revealed in ritual and dance

>To the ancients there were secrets
>shells pried apart to reveal
>women round and pale as the moon
>cloistered and then used

In women there are mysteries
the changing mysteries of the moon
the moon unveiled in our faces
faces sculpted from knowledge and birth

>Priests tried to dike the moon kenning
>and what a woman's body knew
>drained of herblore and inheritance
>lands annexed by church and state

Bound with the earth yet lifted by the moon
we bathe in the moon's silvery soothing light
a light that does not burn but shows the path
a path that any can follow unconcealed

> Built high on righteousness, pyres
> scourged all but fear
> But a tide as red as blood broke through
> wills and voices undammed and surging

The full moon returns healed and whole
We cannot halt this transmutation
inevitable phase of the moon
We wake under the full moon's glow
filled and brimming, witches all

By The Light Of The Moon

By the light of the moon
I stand revealed
Licked smooth, cool glowing
Filled with lunar touch
An alabaster sepulchre
Awaiting the songs
Of eternal night

Tongued to molten silver
The sucking ocean
Beckons

We move to meet
Mercurial drops glue
To marbled skin

Submerged
Only the chill, grey eye
In a noncommittal night
Watches

Penned By My Hand

I entered disguised to give her final test
no threat, she crouched, clasped in iron
her hidden truths torn out
We now waited for confession

> A sword no more can kill
> nor a pen can write
> She laughed a spray
> of blood and teeth

My fingers crossed to save my soul
her glare as searing as the brands
used to bare the secrets she hoarded

> A child cannot be a wren
> but can sing like one
> She hawked up frothy pink
> You're not one of us

I cautiously asked
You mean a witch?
Did she hex?

My feet retreated from her spittle
I brushed dirt and rat droppings
from meticulously tattered robes

> Look around and you tell me
> A carpet cannot weave its pattern
> Her eyes shuttered like an owl's
> It is your hand that holds the pen

Riddles
was she working magic?

Then why on God's earth
did she not charm away her pain?

Book Of Shadows

This is the book whose tales are endless

This spine, worn and fractured, no longer braces
the torn cover, stained, battered threadbare
allure as faded as the title none can read
pages crinkled, pale yellow skin
too thin to hold many words anymore
pages devoured by word-hungry worms
these tales are branded in the souls of survivors

The white hot pincers pierced
deeper than the lore that bound women
extracted teeth and nails and tongues
branded carnage and terror on flesh
The tales, only mindless howls

The purging flames consumed
these ragged weeping tales
seared muscles and eyes and hearts

scorched flesh and blame from bone
The words, only oily red lumps

These tales are inked with clotted blood
enough flowed for the truth left untold
the pages are wrinkled causeways of grief
curled and charred with wordless screams
the title, the unnamed now churned into the
    loam
this cover of flayed flesh harbored human malady
this spine, like the survivors, hardened, shriven
    and broken

This is the book whose shades cry for justice

Broken Words

How can she taste the morning dew
when gore pools where her tongue once lived?

Earth's soft richness
slips from bloodied fingers

>Blood and soil form red clay
>Silence is mortared into the soul

How can she hear the breeze shake leaves
when needles pierce eardrums with silence?

The crisp relief of flowing water
cannot soothe feet caressed by blades

>Needles for sewing stitch words
>and secrets into the flesh

How can she plead with trees that once knew her
when branches are clubs that come for her head?

The forest forgets she plucked sweet comfrey
as her fingers become twigs for the fire

> Nests lie abandoned and burrows unfilled
> friend watches friend with an eye for the odd
> Wood is gathered but not to heat food
> the forest forms walls to hide human purpose

Women stand still, fear freezing their mouths.
Power forms the bond that shackles her wrists.

Who will hear her words now that her body is broken?
The living won't talk and only hear what they wish.

In Feline Grace

I love lying low in long grass
bathe in the sky's wild breath
hide in shadows' light clasp
a fierce prowler watching
waiting, ready to spring
snare unwary with pointed fangs

My claws shift, shortening
from adamantine hardness, resolute
primal action into curled fingers
cringing, grasping for purchase
as boots stomp into ribs, my world
shifts and shakes, tenuous perch
swaying dropping me into
scalding words washing away
confidence and hope

I growl, hiss, swat away
crouch in the suffocating cave
of compliance, lick wounds

until the threat dissipates
alone in sunlight I groom, smoothing
hair, demeanor, determination

I will prove myself predator
free-spirited warrior, proud
when next a hand or foot aims
to damage, take me down
make me less, I will unleash my animal
self, use curved glinting claws
sharp as the blades in my drawer
and draw lines not to cross in red

Loreena

Fire-tressed goddess
hair an aura of light and gold
you sit with harp
of wire and wood quiet
until your touch vibrates the air
shimmers my reality
reshapes it with impassioned hands

Your harpstrings
my heartstrings I sense
fill with laughter and howls
too potent to contain at your touch
fingers pluck strings anew
and joy leaks my tears from within

You sing
angels hold their breath
goddess in your creation
you mold anew the world struck dumb

breathe love into each note
sent flying on winged words

Muse of mortal amber
breathing, being what others dream
you open my doors of flesh
send a light beholden
through you to me

The Briar Witch

The briar witch is winter bound
and often found on icy paths
lets slip her crackly hiemal laugh
to soften all the snowy drifts

She hunkers harvesting briar thatch
sooty reaching branches snare
the ash-dark winter breath in wait
tear a hole for skulking sun and sky

She wanders widdershins scribing circles
rings around the local skating rink
knife sharp as her honed wit she cuts
and carves gnarled pipes and shafts

Into her pipe goes night-dyed herbs
exhales smoke into her incantation
as she chants *Go Manitoba go*
her favorite team for this bonspiel

Thorns are trimmed and saved
for rivals to feel doubt's icy prickle
her breath a fog of curses, words
as cold and hard as burned stones

She scrutinizes a roll, a skip, the sweep
of meticulously threaded briar twigs
into new brooms, a brush, a token
she bestows upon her champions

These are her cheers, her functional luck
for rocks to ride the cleared frozen track
traditional briar brooms create the slide
and bring the lead into the house

She likes to end each ritual match
with keggers and a briar rose
that soothe worries, give sweet dreams
and bind her team to return vows

She will watch the Brier Cup in spring
amongst the blooms and bracken, then plant
broom and prune teams for clean sweeps
and skills to flourish throughout the year

The Hedge Witch

The hedge witch can be found
edging race tracks, calculating the odds

Adorned in hats as big as plates
martinis her elixir as she determines
the future, places polished coins
hedges her bet on this horse, that car
the sleek silver slip of greyhounds
Lady Luck she's been called
a bouquet of flattery by the men
who would rather have her at their sides
than casting lots against them

When fall seeps away to winter's deep
she no longer beats around the bush
the hedge witch retreats and leaves
to her cottage in Hamilton
aligns her fortune, writes enchantments
to dazzle any financial wizard

Then she orders into dormancy
regimental lines of barren hedgerows
With spring she will release their green
check dividends and find the jauntiest hat
to ensure bountiful earnings on her return

The Storm Witch

The storm witch rolls in at any time
day or night, hair a gray twister

She often rumbles across the prairies
from Red Deer to Abbotsford
throttles open, her hog growling
a grin that brings a lightning flash

Her leathers have the power
of all special capes and cloaks, shield
from every curse and road rash
rogue or screaming bible thumper
hides her in the heart of the storm
where she sharpens bolts of light

When she laughs the wind howls
chills braggarts to their marrow
dances a dervish in her hair
speeds her on her rounds
cruising the Trans Canada

COLLEEN ANDERSON

In fall, she brews grains and hops
potions to steel suspect nerves
but on occasion she distills
her special magical blend
mixed with Canadian Club burning a path
straight to every heart on a pyre
where wildfire passions rampage
and victims obey her desires
any drink the storm witch dispenses
always a tempest with no teacup

Men and women forgo tempered thoughts
go mad for her, chasing dreams
she needs no weapon; the pool cue
her wand for deflecting hurled insults
or creating lurid visions
when she distributes cold justice
inclement weather, shocking revelations
of partners infidelities, or a hidden cheat

Her divinations bring her money
in games of love or waiting out the weather
any attempt to subdue
tame the roving ways
brings a hail of words, a thunderous roar
turbulent, chilly relationships
flashes of ire whiteout everything for days
where she freezes the brashest souls
ice statues that wait for spring thaws

I DREAMED A WORLD

The storm witch moves on
as suddenly as she arrives
loud and proud, she fears none
brings balance in bluster
then sleeps as the pressure lightens
liaisons melt away
calm descends, a pause to gather resources
she will wait for summer's heat-laden lull
return with a vengeance none withstand
and electrify lives with vitality
that will last for months to come

The Sand Witch

From coast to coast
she is found combing her hair
beaches for bones, bottle caps
glass buffed to a matte veneer

She rides driftwood out among the shoals
returns with tangled seaweed tresses
salty spume upon her lips
Her sojourns are a mystery
part of her constant drive
to conjure mist and sirens
calm the sea that pounds the coast

The sand witch likewise settles
on Victoria's shore or Sandy Cove's
She favors worn blues, tempest greens
stormy gray, the surf tickling her toes
Her tools are net, paddle, knife and awl
a bowl of smoked salmon, mayo and bread
as pebbled with grains as the sand beneath

I DREAMED A WORLD

Summer is her season as she makes a feast
strings sand dollars, shells and hollowed crabs
to ward against trawling dogs and ants
a clattering lure to becalmed cats
that hope to lap tuna tidepools
and other ebbing jetsam
Castoffs are her specialty, lost souls
and wandering strays gathered in
her incandescent net

As the sun sinks towards its watery bed
she drags in lonely sailors from the bay
hears their plaintive calls
the cries of gulls
feeds them hearty sandwiches always kept on
    hand

Set free to drift, they will return
when she pries apart Davy's locker
uses coastal margarine and some briny delight
to fill their bellies and weigh them down
pluck the pearl of their desires
upon the sand, anchoring them
to her cause, and lunches in the bay

What Goldilocks Learned

Beautiful and dyed blond
I moved out to explore the forest
a lumberjack beckoned
Once inside his cottage I didn't notice
all was dished out
and everything in its place

That first man was a boor
he sawed and hammered and nailed
Did I have to spread my legs
try to mend the cleaving
when he said I hadn't pleased him in bed?

Too hard, too self-centered.
                                          I had to leave.

The second one was a bore
pasty as porridge
he lectured as internet chat filled his head

I DREAMED A WORLD

Me, only a hairdresser, no experience, no
   degree
where would I end up?

Too soft, too condescending.
                              I had to leave.

By the third I thought I had chosen just right
Not too hard or too soft
Not too noncommittal or too passionate
cleaning up after kids, feeding everyone
Knowing the place of everything
even me, was more than I could bear

Shorn of golden sun reflecting
essentially bare
I left the taste of what had been
No longer seeking flavors
or trying to fit what looks just right
I have chosen freedom to be as I please

A Good Catch

She had never been a good wife
staying out till all hours
coming home wet and wild
with flesh stuck between her teeth

She had fallen for his best lines
reeled him in, netted a husband
After marriage she dropped the camouflage
became a bit of a disappointment

When she joined the band she found her place
forgot for awhile who she was
rattling spoons over her scales
and singing of shipwrecked loves

She stopped looking at other men
remained mute upon the rocks
traded her shell bras for ones of lace
sailors watching still ran aground

I DREAMED A WORLD

Perhaps she needs to try again, harder
loving words are bait enough
but pearls last longer when held in the hand
her husband but a shoal against the sea's allure

She had tried to be a good wife cooking
calmly stirring the bowl's contents
but she couldn't help dip the spoon and lick it
add pepper to fish heads and fingers

Not all sirens give warnings but she will
write a note on handmade, scented paper
will not eat her love but leave him
with fishwife memories when the ocean calls

Mermaid's Comb

She pulls the teeth through her hair
a gentle tug, a subtle chewing
of seaweed and kelp
untangling stray fingers from her last catch

It's not an easy life swimming to and fro
searching for wrecks upon the rocks
She often played her hair like a harp
wishing for more than sinking fellows
or treasures to larder her sea-trenched chests

She yearned to taste something new
to see beyond the seaweed haul
do more than nibble sailors to death
add their ribs and finger bones
to the collar about her neck

Sparkling coins, the winking eyes
of gems nothing but aquatic litter

gaudy encrustations no longer
netting her attention in boring marine games

But what can a girl of fin, scales and flesh do
caught between two worlds
cool calm unfettered depths swept away
the other of dry and bright reaches
where clarity always wins

She combs again her sea-tossed tresses
untangling her life, her loves
her dreams half-formed as pearls
being spun in their shells

Her world changes with the tides
ebbs and flows as does her every whim
discarded when the surge recedes
leaving shells and seaweed
the rejected bodies of men

She eyes the distant moon-skimmed shores
pulls her comb through her hair
and with mirror and siren song
lures women now into her lair

Mermaid

We mate—slippery, instinctual
wet bodies writhe
his crucifix, wound on a chain about his neck
    falls
into my open mouth trawling
hooking, catches my lip, my tongue
rolls about the dulled, golden barb
I gasp as he plunges down
rise up as he pulls back
he plays me skillfully until I lash out
sweaty droplets frenzy his flesh and mine
I clutch and hold and thrash about
not yet ready to be free

Undulations exhalations
we are pulled into waves
crescendo   crash
cresting high—we reach new depths then

I DREAMED A WORLD

Exhausted I fall back
the waves subside
he pulls out   away   a tide
that leaves and returns

The Mermaid

(*villanelle*)

She slips beyond the reach of man
in torpid heat he kneels to pray
bright-eyed, fevered upon the sand

He casts hook and line with firm hand
in frothing water day by day
she slips beyond the reach of man

He feels the curse as if a brand
the distant gods regard his face
bright-eyed, fevered upon the sand

Sleek siren heeds no human plan
from ships, or sailors' longing gaze
she slips beyond the reach of man

Bright silver lures her near the strand
the man has hardened in his ways
bright-eyed, fevered upon the sand

I DREAMED A WORLD

The man must feed his hungry clan
pulls food not myth from raging waves
She slips beyond the reach of man
bright-eyed, fevered upon the sand

Heart Of Glass

While my blood flowed warm and red
covered by flesh as white as snow
your heart ran slow and cold
sheathed by a rigid iron will

It was always about the heart
yours chiseled of frosted glass
long before you gazed in that magic mirror
recognized your spiteful stare could freeze the
    world

Nothing could shatter your diamond hard need
puncture your hate, no slivers of glass or
    needles
to stitch a heart on your sleeve or back into a
    body
as devoid of empathy as of love

You sent another to do your dirty work
hoping to spread the wintering of your domain
but it's hard to stopper compassion's wellspring

and a kind word pierces a heart truer than
    arrows

So like you to tear out hearts with words that kill
with hopes to eat my laughter, devour my youth
make me as dead as your feelings had become
and bury any guilt with proclamations of your
    right

You found beauty in others distracting,
    covetous
unless you were the center of adoration
eventually they enclosed me in crystal
a chrysalis to preserve me from the poison you
    spewed

In my death your realm was still ice and isolation
but nature has a way of balancing hate and love
those who mourned planted me in their hearts
so that I could return anew, inevitable as the
    seasons

If you had only broken through the glass coffin
    of your fear
used the shards to carve a way back into the
    world
let the pain flow until your blood was clear, your
    breath light
then together we could have grown old, laughing

Hearts beating in tandem with the rhythm of the seasons
as we marveled at the melting of the snow white realm

I Dreamed A World

Everyone must sleep at the end of the era
It is the only way that thoughts fly free
making patterns, a new weave
I had to be the template
the apex of the royal line
heir and loom of changes to come

But nothing is instantaneous
Not love not change
nor the turning of the world's wheel
So wheel and spindle it was that spun
into a realm of sleep of make believe
of imagining my freedom

I dreamed a world where days unravel
    predictably
curses by mad half-women have no weight
and fear of a spindle prick is only for the pain

No uttered prophesy fringes a birthday with
 dread
nor magic from the craft of one's hands
and the only spell is one of making

I dreamed a world where love's blossom has few
 thorns
All choices made on waking are with full
 knowledge
of my desires and patterns for my future
are woven of my own designs
Arranged marriages are only made
when all the parties agree

I dreamed a world where princesses have voices
beyond singing from their gilded rooms
and beauty whether sleeping or awake
is not for sale or inheriting lands
Decisions to plant something new twine
respect for intellect and innovation

Worlds are imperfect things
and dreams are circumspect
their stories running counterpoint to logic
warp and weft difficult to disentangle as briar
 roses

I awoke to find my world consists of one day at a
 time
Half-mad I've grown with menial drudgery
for what else can a disinherited princess do

I Dreamed a World

My dreams and wishes fall on disenchanted air
No craft of mine is better than that of
    machinations
and the only spell is how to succeed

I awoke to find love is distanced by an apparatus
making a one-night stand unfulfilling
as a prince's demand for loyalty if not for love
My choices are limited to who might return my
    call
and arranged meetings are only made
for sex without a need for courting

I awoke to find every girl a princess
demanding the latest fashion as women
smear concocted potions, unguents, dire pastes
and try magics to hold time at bay
I have tried to nurture the shoot of new
    beginnings
but find it strangled out by greed

Everyone must sleep to escape the nightmares
of the day, to pretend we soar higher
away from a life that pricks us
I made a mistake using the last zephyrs
of magic to dream a simple desire
lacking complexity that living really means

Nothing is easy
not love not change

nor the turning of our lives
So I dream of the welcoming narcotic jab
that will spin me into a realm of dreams of hope
of imagining freedom

Cinderella's Pumpkin

After the prince satisfied his quest
installing my dainty foot
in the mink shoe he married
me added to his collection

Those long lonely days
as my transformation took place
mice and lizards my fey staff
a pumpkin transmuted into a coach
and pair, rags to glamour

After all, we met on looks alone
my bedazzlement with influence
more than I could use dissipated
once I had a chance to think
to take a breath, loosen my corset

The prince moved away
on kingdom needs, another quest

or a dragon lady to bind
I had been a machine dumping ashes
sifting cinders, baking, scouring
a perfect world for the privileged

I itched to bring order
to a palace already in its place
every servant jealously guarding
their realm of right and duty

In boredom I contacted my enchanted guardian
but not for gowns nor enthralling
trysts with dashing rulers
this time I wished to change again, take flight
learn the skills of riding out of reach

Another gourd became my sedan
a race into the country
against the dragging time
to save my life for a day
with russet foxes and dormice
my new and feral attendants
always maintaining an uncultivated glint
in the depths of their eyes
my heart

I raced the trees through the passage
of endless repetition to find
a space where I could be
I lost the track of appointments

and trails until I ran wild
in a field of rodents and vixens
kicking along a great orange pumpkin

Women often seem to run afoul
of curses, witches and evil stepmothers
living under the demands of one
or the other until virtue wins
a place in a man's world

I ran through meadows
punting the gourd with my petite
yet sturdy peasant feet
until a man named Peter
found me in his field
He understands the land
the grains, the woodland mede
the need to touch the earth
feel the fecund thrills of growth

When he noticed my feet
it was not because of rare furs
that encased them nor of a size
that denoted something to protect
a delicate keepsake for within castle walls

But how my toes gripped the soil
that I outran his greyhound
We laughed in the crescent moonlight
shadows danced as we chased the pumpkin

skittering helter skelter
until a tree delivered its demise

It took the rupturing fruit
its scent infused us with a need
to dig into the deep dark loam
burrow like feasting worms
crawl beneath the leaves

I left behind a perfect life
to live with a farmer
but when they say he kept me
very well it means he won't take
the king's rubies nor sacks of gold
knows I own my self, free to leave
whenever my feet demand

Snow White's Apples

A bulimic knows
there are two ways to consume
one is not to eat at all
the other, take the world
into yourself sins, joys, pains
the full sensory experience
but not grow fat on it but purge again
and again... for balance, feel despair
so that joy is all the richer
when devoured guiltlessly again

Starved for love or a word of praise
Snow White sought out something to fulfill
took the path of runaways, of precocity
of survivors from broken homes
not all girls who run endure or find peace
she managed lodgings with men of splintery mien
striving to be gentlemen all the same

but good intentions and preordained destinies
can still go astray

In hunger to fill a need, hide her shame
Snow White was tempted by an apple
the oldest crop seeded in memory
a blush of thought on the tree of life
or abundant knowledge of good and evil
she saw in the mirror, the roseate lie
herself a hybrid queen filled with envy
who tried to join the halves together
obliterate the exposed bruised side

Those apples had special weight
ever since time began
the first fruit a sweet tease leaving
the bitter aftertaste from the core
a weighty illicit craving, a dark desire
for savoring a beginning neverending
for going beyond safe borders

How could she resist
in the end her wish bloomed true
the desire of all who seek eternity
an apple poisoned with all of time
Snow White bit and chewed and choked
then fell into a suspended world
that her predecessor had long known
a goddess once, who may have dropped
just as windfall apples do
from the wind's lecherous touch

Idunn of the golden apples won hard
harvester's knowledge and full of power
she never punished, only rewarded the gift
that kept on giving, endless life, youth, beauty
Gods grow bored when millennia pass
Idunn and the Norse sailed onto other realms
leaving a distillation, an elixir
a breath of remembering in the apples of
    Midgard

Fairy tales are the memories of gods long gone
wishes of mortals for what can never be
Snow White frozen in her world of in-between
received the eternal gift but not as it once had
    been
She was stuck between the realms
neither dead nor alive, preserved for all time
until the day some random prince
heimliched her back to life

She has spent an eternity sandwiched
into film and print, but wanting neither
immortalized yet seeking always seeking
an apple that will give her a taste
of a love that's not foreseen
that destiny cannot touch, something natural
that happens on a whim
like apples falling from a tree

The Looking Glass

Revealed as volcanic glass and deep lakes
the pin-dot speck of contemplation
from the human eye, the mirror imitates
by way of vanity, Celts polished brass
enough to reflect their glories
when the sun shone auspiciously

Egyptians, Greeks, Phrygians
all have walked forward
to peer at their image, know themselves
gazing into pools, brass, copper and
gleaming pieces of glass, then backed by silver
the looking glass revealed one's true worth
the color of one's mien even if not golden

Long after Narcissus was ensnared
his lovely guise rippling in a pond
Alice found a mystical gateway mirror
phased through and fell into awakening

while Snow White was a victim of conspiracies
when a prophetic mirror dared to dictate the
    future
the fear of seven years or an eternity of bad luck

Alice took the invitation to dive
into her inner self slide past
the sharp-edged stern upbringing
discover ferocious roses, rampant cards
and a crazed, demanding queen
crammed into her underworld

Snow White's red queen lived beyond
the mirror, never truly looked within
but glared at tapestries woven with dreams
visions of chastity, immortal youth
neither of which she could achieve again
except through sorcerous envy

If you asked her, she would say
it was all for Snow White's good and growth
to give her depth, to strengthen virtues
as she lay bound in faceted crystal
a reliquary that let her look upon the world
but never touch it through the glass

Alice chose while Snow White was pushed
neither expected the twisted inside-out world
the mirror's shards cut a path between
two lands, one where blood flows from the cut

for a looking glass is not a window
looking in nor looking out

Mirrors are one way only, looking forward
no matter how we peer into the past
wishing, dreaming for what once was
they reflect lives passing by, moving on
Alice and Snow White blindly took the leap
onto a spark of light that continues to the future

Learning To Run

Shoes have always been vehicles
They began with fitting me for a journey
An elegant veneer, like glass, like mink
That transported me to a fantasy féte

When the curfew fell I fled
A breadcrumb trail replaced with a shoe
A clue for the prince who followed
Looking for the one that got away

Those court shoes galvanized my stepsisters
Mutilation the fad as they sawed and hacked
What they lacked—tiny feet to fit the trend
And unadorned were the feats of hard work

Shoes can be prisons, confining one's nature
Gentle diligence and loyalty remained
Hollow as an abandoned slipper that led
To my capture gilded in gold, azure silk,
    brocade

I am a kept woman closeted with collections
Confections, sapphires, rubies and pomades
Shelved and viewed for special occasions
Until I tear off my shoes to run free

Charmed

Someday my prince will come
Someday my prince will come…

I've been sitting in this ivory tower
this frozen palace, entwined bower
weaving threads, gnawing bones
waiting for a prince to take me home

I'm not allowed to sniff the flowers
shop or take sensual showers
my fingers aren't supposed to roam
across my body's erogenous zones

Wait a minute!
I'm tired of waiting all the time
prattling out this asinine rhyme

Someday my prince *will* come
So when I get him and I will
I always do—it's foreordained

he's going to have to keep me entertained

He better be the best
with a magic wand
that will make *me* come all night
shoot for the stars
I don't want just any prince
if one is all I can have

After all, we must live happily ever after and let me tell you
faery godmothers, magic frogs, fancy shoes
or enchanted dishwashers will not content me for long
I mean really, would you marry some fellow who thinks a kiss
is a marriage made in heaven?
Known as Prince Charming only lasts till the wedding vows

On second thought, if I can leave this tale as it is, perhaps I'll take the bumpkin down the road with a 9 to 5 job. More likely I'll have to support him. Hmmm, perhaps I'll just keep the tower, go strata, invest in real estate, bring in a computer and home entertainment system. I'll leave the princes and the frogs— indeed! Horny toads may have more value and with them you know what you're going to get.

Shahrazad: Captive Passion

You only know the stories. Hear the climax of tales begun to stay the sharp kiss of your curved blade.

Like time's sunrise I had beheld you, Shah. Your love tarnished by your queen you searched to love a woman who could do no wrong. For one day, each had wept or pleaded. At daybreak you silenced each bride, acclaimed her sister to seduction. Your rage swept away more than flesh.

I watched your people retreat into darkened homes, lock daughters away like gems from your gaze. So I sought to stop you, asked my father to set my destiny, sure that I could hold you with the stories I would forge.

That first night you spilled my new blood like the ruby wives who had gone before. The perfume of their thoughts lingered on pillows stained with tears. At dawn I promised you words to fill your emptiness.

By day I fed on ancient tales, grand deaths and past lives. Silence clung so thickly that the moon too, in its approach, begged from my lips words to stifle its loneliness. I spilled words as impassioned as a kiss upon your mind.

I released the nightly tales, brushing air with soft wings of their worlds. Jealous for your touch, I longed to keep you captive. I suspended each tale over the brazier of your wonder, burnished to glowing amber as though to sear me. I became a pond, stretched my limbs beneath you, and pulled you in.

I left you feeding my own hope. The death bird perched upon my shoulder now rarely caught my notice. I dreaded only the day you would fly from me. My desire held its tongue while I told endless tales, and sculpted men clothed in your form.

Well past the six hundredth I bore you a child, the fruit of so many words. As if it was the unleashed ifrit, you watched my every move.

How long had you waited for my tales to become flesh and bone and blood? I cursed the making of the words for the chains they had become. You provided beggars with bread and fruit, helped the lame to beds, but for me, they were only stories too.

Sunny days and silk curtains fluttered across my room. Upon the cushions I whispered to the ghost wives whose pungent memories endured. Always you returned from your people. It was the eunuchs who said the people cheered your justice, yet as you passed awe stilled their words, for fear you would notice the teller, not the tales.

This night is two nights past a thousand. I sever all links. As I abandon these words I suspect my time with you means nothing but distraction. I longed now only wish an ending to these tales. I welcome its kiss, the curved blade against my skin.

I stop now, wearied, emptied of what you crave. As the last sound falls, there is nothing left but truth, my naked need that you have not read.

As I Sleep

She lies upon me as I sleep
And lets her fingers around me creep
Oh yes, and presses them quite deep

I dream that she lies quite still
At one with me to bide her time
But as the days grow less bold
She shifts and sighs with weary cold

I dream her breath is soft and warm
Yet hides an underlying chill
Her only sounds are snaps and groans
But mute I hope she will go home

I dream she holds me close and tight
And as her whispers blanket me
I try to leave yet must remain
They lace the Arctic in my veins

I DREAMED A WORLD

I dream her fingers seek me out
Dig in, and burrow till I scream
And roots like ice suck numb my shell
Her freezing force won't let me wake

Winter lies upon me as I weep
And wraps me in a shroud of sleep
Oh yes, and presses me quite deep

Uninvited

They call uninvited
When everything's a mess
Windows are smudged grey
And I will not see their faces
Walls curtain out their voices
Quietly I breathe
No one was expected
My life's in disarray
My papers are not straightened
I'm too busy for such guests
Another day is needed
At least to tidy up
They will not stop their banging
Refuse to heed my hint
The house is left in shadow
Because the Valkyries have called

A Strange Attraction

He's a General.
Rules Star systems they say
    Scowls storms above
    3-inch inset fangs.
    Bracelets orbit elbows,
    Rings enforce his brows,
    Paprika hair floats to his waist—
    Adds a promise of bloodshed
    Rather than civility.
Two rows from me, a cadet faints
    From the arrow of his gaze.
A sheep-like rustle brushes the ranks—
Crystalline fears of his command.
    Noticed, he closes the distance
Between us like a battle-cruiser
Swallowing its enemy.
    No falter in stance, his eyes
    Probe my soul.
    You're not frightened, he says.

No, just repulsed.
        Indignity burns his eyes red.
A collective gasp vacuums the air
From the room.
        He asks, why do you cater death?
I answer, why do you court ugliness?
    Repulsed, we become lovers.

The Traveler

She haunted smoky train stations
towing a tattered, overlarge suitcase
like a faithful dog more streetwise
than innocence held close like her shawl

The stations were any station, everywhere
people discarding used secrets, fleeing from
   their past
the lost foraged where others had devoured any
   happy endings
There, she was no different, except she
   rekindled hope

Gifting smiles, no scars or wrinkles mapped her
   face
her eyes like pools one falls into but cannot
   escape
not the flowing font of knowledge nor a grail to
   behold

She was the stone that water cannot touch but surrounds

Passersby noticed her diminutive frame, the monolithic valise
yet forgot her as she trundled away, the case swaying a rhythm
crammed with mysteries and castoffs of the most unlikely lives
She hummed a tune, childlike, light as pigeons in the girders overhead

It was only late into the night, in the clutches of old doorways
leaning on the broken teeth of railings
that she would unzip her bag, furrow like a ferret
reveal the burdens that she had taken and stored

Sometimes she pulled out a chipped, porcelain tea set
shared a biscuit and the contents of her travels
with the Gypsies or the Wandering Jew
any who flowed unnoticed through the stream of time

She savored each lost soul, every sorrowed past
as if they were all that kept her going
as she journeyed to the next station
waiting for the departed and forgotten

Voodoo Doll

Be my voodoo doll
by moonlight let me stick you with pins
write notes in arcane symbols
etching my love into your skin
Let me dance and sing to the stars
the qualities you possess that I will too
I'll cast a spell so you'll love me well

Be my voodoo doll
silence you'll keep as I stitch your lips
sealing your kiss forever inside
Immortal I'll make you when I pack you with
    rags
switch your eyes for glass gems
a watch for your faithless tick tock heart
you and I will never be apart

Be my voodoo doll

Patchwork Girl

I stitched on my leg
after he tore it off
unhappy that I could stand on my own

He blackened my eye
didn't want me to see
the women threaded around his loins
like the heads of warriors taken in battle

I washed and rinsed
patted on a foundation able to adapt
to bruised views
Rose colored glasses couldn't help me

He stabbed me through and through
Blood paling to nacre
a shell I built to contain the severed pieces

He cut me off from society
Dismembered my compassion but in the process

his creation, like Dr. Frankenstein's
was more than he bargained for

I've grown adept at sewing
making patterns, fine even lines
When anyone looks closely
they only see a doll

I am more than the sum of my parts
more than a carcass left hanging
Every stitch has a beginning and an end
Made with the sharp bite of the metal thorn
I made myself into something new

I cut and repatterned, used the tools
I had grown used to
unraveled him vein by vein
sinew by sinew leaving a trail
A warning, not to take the same path
use the same patterns

The Beetle Wife

She organizes, mindlessly
scurrying back and forth
bringing in groceries, creating lunches
filing, ensuring all things ordered
sometimes it seems she's rolling shit uphill
when no one watches she stretches
an extra set of legs, pretends to dance
yet worries discovery means more work

She clicks her teeth
a hard rasp, mandibles to cut
her frustration, dirty clothes on beds
soiled dishes on counters, ties
to obligations, her self unattended
the reasons he can't paint, or clean or love
she may as well be a bug, a beetle
for all she gets underfoot

I DREAMED A WORLD

She is good, so very good
staying in line, following the rules
they don't notice her eyes watching
everything, the many facets
as she sits so very very still, pinned
as if under glass, inspecting every grain
the small secrets under the bed
tucked in a pocket, hidden in an external
    account

She has her own secret
wedged beneath her strong chitin shell
the beautiful clothes her city camouflage
feelings shielded from a careless brushoff
how she's kept her hopes, desires to change
release erotic dreams burrowed away
and most of all her wish to be alive
not just a jewelled makech on a chain

Some day soon she will spread protective elytra
drop the guise that she cares
reveal her inner self, the vestigial heart
stretch out her wings, fly high
into the woods, a city, another home
where she will change, be seen
for what she is, no longer hide her strength
and what she will become

Talesen's Trap 2115-2135: Maie

Months wasted,
canned and chewing chalky paste
before you landed our lives.
Eternal waiting
until hydroponics functioned
and environment analyzed.

At least the air was breathable
gravity remained as
tenuous as tempers.
Outside contained invisible foes,
you later met.

Six—we formed the colony;
came to know each other.
Too well the knowing
like families sometimes are.

I DREAMED A WORLD

Three months in a claustro-compound
before we could explore.
Three long, lunar months.

Tensions taut we orbited
each other's anger.
We argued exploration
vented black hole despair.
Moved to solo thoughts
you travelled planet's darkside.
Said you'd return late.

I—we waited.
Time passed
in time.
We accepted your loss
our loss.

Time flew a jagged orbit.

Late
you returned
and saw separation's price.
You, the same as the day you left
trapped twenty years apart
from us.
We, the aged memories
you had missed
shocked by your youth.

Talesen's Trap 2203-2213: Thena

Ten days of toil
on a tortured planet of 5 G's.
Each movement costs a meal
that's sucked up every 2 hours.
Skin sags in pockets,
restoration will come later.

Ten days—for a military victory
on a planet light-years distant.
Itchy sweat and pain
our only companions.

Ten days pay—not worth our aging.
We return for regeneration,
find the war has stopped.
No one remembers us,
as if we were statues.

I DREAMED A WORLD

Ten days we were gone
fighting an old war,
while everyone lives a peace
that's lasted ten years.

Talesen's Trap 2272-2378: Demey

After the wars
they said we'd settle
Talesen for more than minerals;
Sprout life from
shifting gravity and time pockets.

We settled each pocket,
but live as separate planets.
Distant neighbors orbit
our lives, never in contact,
but visible, static.

Krona stepped from thick syrup
timestreams to ours.
The same age as my son
though born centuries
before his two decades.
Love entwined them back to Krona's time.

Talesen traps us.
My son moves as brick
the image of what he was
those twenty, thirty, years gone.

He returns for an unknown goodbye.
At my side he weeps,
but it was only last week
that I turned from you.
My life flickers away
in the blink of his eye.

Talesen's Trap 3480: Lazu

I am the last.
My people left so long
so long.
In shifting blurs they left,
I stayed—
farmed erratic time.
Plundered Talesen left enough for one
but little for the many.

At first all was quiet
for a year, maybe two.
Then others returned
to caress artifacts,
watch a relic—me.
Daily, seekers arrived
then left within hours.
To them, a month had passed
in time lost, staring on Talesen.

I am the last
but not yet old.
I have outlived
their ships, their lives.
In their precious records
I have lived millennia.
The curator of their cultures,
eternal watcher of past dreams.

But time's the same.
My immortality is hollow.

Nocturne Expire

Succulent succubus
you lick at my mind.
My veins throb
and trailing nails burn
ice through my soul.
It's deadly, yes, to succumb to you
infernal amour, terrible desire.
But the ardor you unleash,
unearthly, devouring,
I've never felt this before.
Your diamond claws pull
red tremors through my flesh
and hair like frenzied snakes
lashes my face.
A pale ember before,
my life flares through every pore.
I would rather spend it all within you
then leave it a cooled chunk of despair.
I erupt, soul floods molten womb.

You laugh a sensuous ripple, complete
and retreat, withdraw, my essence entombed.
You fade into air.
Forlorn
I cry, don't go.
My limbs grow numb
and I end ecstatic, calm.

The Price

I dreamt again of being Aubera.

The moon clothed my skin in a pall of white,
And Shaylyn's clothed in amber.
We prepared the nectar—Lossun.
Hands crushing fragrant pods
mixed with fats of sacrificed krae.
Shaylyn, solemnly smearing paste
along her arm's dark curves,
her mind cocooned in her role—
Together Aubera
at the shadowing of the suns—
The crux of Shonun Dark.

As children we had grown
in passive study of what would be.
Games and rolling in the sands.
Molded for one future day too distant.
Nothing but a whispered promise:

I DREAMED A WORLD

You will be the ones—Aubera.
Saviours at the crux of Shonun Dark.

Infused, aglow from the Elderbane bloom
Shaylyn and I—
Devising special rituals.
None but she and I
and the Corun priests knew.
We would break the grip of Kinderfell.

I dream of being Aubera again,
with Shaylyn.
Her seed-black eyes staring
at the chasm that ripped the world asunder
And I, holding, clasping her hand.
Aubera held Corun's faceted eye,
collected rays of the dual suns.
The last of Shonun Bright.

Together, Shaylyn and I—Aubera.
Opposites and the same.
Two into one.
The world held whole within our hands.
And no one knew the outcome.
The world once old, made new again.
Aubera blending life and death—
blood and tears, chants and silence.

I dream, and see again
the crux of Shonun Dark.

Chaining words together, signing sigils
and ripping petals from the Elderbane.
The world cracked and writhed around Aubera
wombing us as one.

Kinderfell.
Sacrifice and offering.
In the light and shadow
fires birthed.

Aubera halved to one.
Only Bere emerged, only I.

My role completed, of long days reciting,
gripping Shaylyn with eyes in fever-light—
the remembered chants.
I am new-born after, yet unwhole.

I dream of Shaylyn and being Aubera.

Oh You!

Oh, you beautiful doll
you great big beautiful doll
you're a penthouse, playboy icon
sweet enough to give the boys a hard on
with your airbrushed limbs in Vogue
and skin of face-lift elastic
rocket breasts as smooth as silicon
you're the genuine plastic beauty doll

Oh,
you're such a doll
everyone wants to be just like you
a regular dress up, pink prom, prissy prim
barbie doll
oh, honey baby doll, you're my pliable
chatty Kathy doll
a sexy rubber, blow-up doll
you beautiful, beautiful doll

Doll, they say we can't live without you
in splatter films or skin flicks
with bloody legs and arms askew
irresistible you're dressed to kill
cream dream such a scream
to be cleaved and raped
and gashed and reamed
a cut up regular doll

But,
you're just a doll!
a great big beautiful doll
let me wrap your arms about me
you're unreal, not taken seriously
there's no harm in make-believe
you really know just how to please
oh, oh, oh, oh!
oh you beautiful doll

By The End

By the fifteenth month of the drought
the lake no longer hid her secrets
dried out husks littered the silt
trails leading away
mysteries moving to the treeline

She surveyed the carnage
mother nature's vicious attack
search and destroy on her calculated sowing
small organic treasures she had sunk
like naval mines beneath the surface

The drought was not predicted
heat waves swathed her mission directive
the aquatic spawn chose evolution
preferring adaptation to a foreign climate
over certain sunbaked death

By the sixteenth month only dust remains
her belly hollowed, the soil devoid of promise
her food source now devours the people
the ship outfitted for a new system
she makes her hasty exit

Acknowledgements

Writing is a craft that does not spring up instantaneously but comes from work, research, experience, dedication and support. Thank you to all the publishers who saw fit to put these poems into print.

Thank you also to MJae Sydney and the Lycan Valley crew for publishing this collection. Thank you to FJ Bergmann and to Angela Yuriko Smith who have said such kind words about my writing.

COLLEEN ANDERSON

Credits

- A Good Catch, *Poetry Nook* 188th contest, 2019, *Tailfins and Sealskins*, Three Drops from a Cauldron Press, 2016, *Polu Texni*, 2011
- A Question of The Grail, *The Round Table*, 1987
- A Strange Attraction, Amazing Stories, 1990, Chizine, 2001, Stars as Seen From this Particular Angle of Night, 2003
- As I Sleep, *Burning Maiden* Vol. 2, Evil Eye Books, 2015
- Book of Shadows, *Devolution Z*, Issue 8, 2016
- Broken Words, *The Cascadia Subduction Zone* Vol. 10, #1, 2020
- By the End, James Gunn's Ad Astra #7, 2019
- By the Light of The Moon, *Silver Apple Branch*, 1988
- Calliope's Song, *On Spec*, 1993
- Charmed, *Strange Fictions*, Vagabondage Press, 2018

- Cinderella's Pumpkin, *Polu Texni*, 2018
- Cleopatra, *Illumen* Spring 2020, 2020
- Cosmos, *Golden Isis*, 1993
- Father's Child, *Polu Texni*, 2013
- Finding Dionysus, *Crucible*, Barton College, 2009
- Geomystica, *Eternal Haunted Summer*, Summer, 2017
- Heart of Glass, *Polu Texni*, 2013
- I Dreamed A World, *Polu Texni*, 2015
- Illuminating Thoughts, *Polu Texni*, 2013
- In Feline Grace, *Illumen*, 2021
- Learning to Run, *Polar Borealis* #7, 2018
- Loreena, *Color Wheel* #6 Goddess\Muse, 1993
- Masquerade, *OnSpec* #115, Vol. 31 No. 1, 2020
- Medusa, *Burning Maiden* Vol. 2, Evil Eye Books, 2015
- Mermaid, Justousroux.com, 2007
- Mermaid's Comb, *The Future Fire* #45, 2018
- Morrigan's Song, *Heroic Fantasy Quarterly* #24, 2015
- New Age, *Arts and* Crafts *News,* Burnaby Arts Council, 1988, *Color Wheel*-#6 Goddess/Muse, 1993
- Nocturne Expire, *Daughter of Dangerous Dames*, Twilight Tales, 2000, Erotic Fantasy: Tales of the Paranormal, 2004
- Of the Corn: Kore's Innocence, *Witches & Pagans* #21, 2010
- Oh You!, *Maple Tree Literary Supplement* #21, 2016

- Patchwork Girl, *The Future Fire* #37, 2016
- Penned by My Hand, *The Cascadia Subduction Zone* Vol. 10, #1, 2020
- Persephone Dreams, *Eternal Haunted Summer*, Summer 2015
- Queen of Heaven and Earth, *Eternal Haunted Summer*, 2012
- Rapunzel and Medusa, *Polu Texni*, 2017
- Safekeeping, *Cosmic Unicorn*, 1995
- Shahrazad: Captive Passion, *Stars as Seen From this Particular Angle of Night*, 2003, Daughter of Dangerous Dames, Twilight Tales, 2000
- Snow White's Apples, *Polu Texni*, 2020
- Spinning Wheel, *The Cascadia Subduction Zone* Vol. 10, #1, 2020
- Spirit of Heart, *Z Miscellaneous*, 1988
- Talesen's Traps #1, *Ancient Tales, Grand Deaths & Past Lives*, Chapbook Kelp Queen Press, 2001
- Talesen's Traps #2: Thena, *Starline* #2, Vol. 11, 1988
- Talesen's Traps #3, Ancient Tales, Grand Deaths & Past Lives, Chapbook, 2001
- Talesen's Traps #4, *Ancient Tales, Grand Deaths & Past Lives*, Chapbook, Kelp Queen Press, 2001
- The Beetle Wife, *Polu Texni*, 2019
- The Briar Witch, *Eye to the Telescope* #32, 2019
- The Enlightened, *Polar Borealis* #5, 2018

- The First Taste, *Dreams & Nightmares*, 2008
- The Hedge Witch, *OnSpec* #101, Vol. 27. No. 2 Summer 2015, 2016
- The Looking Glass, *Illumen Spring*, 2020
- The Loving Cup, *Golden Isis*, 1993
- The Mermaid, *Spirit's Tincture* #2, 2016, *Polu Texni*, 2012
- The Price, *Starline* #4 Vol. 15, 1992
- The Sand Witch, *Balticon Program* Book, 2nd place, 2018
- The Storm Witch, *Eternal Haunted Summer*, Winter 2019
- The Traveler, *Strange Fictions*, Vagabondage Press, 2018
- The Vernal Queen, *Mythic Circle*, 1989
- Three's the Charm, *Songs of Eretz*, Spring 2020
- Uninvited, *Starline* #4 Vol. 14, 1991
- Visitation: Leda's Lament, *HWA Poetry Showcase II*, 2015
- Voodoo Doll, *Grievous Angel*, 2017
- What Goldilocks Learned, *American Diversity Report*, 2020
- Witch Moon, *The Future Fire* #42, 2017

About The Author

Colleen Anderson is a Canada Council and BC Arts Council grant recipient for writing and has performed her work before audiences in the US, UK and Canada. She enjoys editing, and co-edited Canadian anthologies *Playground of Lost Toys*, *Tesseracts 17*, and her solo anthology *Alice Unbound: Beyond Wonderland*. She has served on Stoker Award and British Fantasy Award juries, and guest edited SFPA's Eye to the Telescope. Colleen currently serves on the board of the Science Fiction and Fantasy Poetry Association (SFPA) and is a member of the Horror Writers Association.

www.ingramcontent.com/pod-product-compliance
Lightning Source LLC
Chambersburg PA
CBHW060359080526
44583CB00012B/384